PrayerStarters

To Help You Heal After Loss

Text © 1999 by Elizabeth Stalling
Published by One Caring Place
Abbey Press
St. Meinrad, Indiana 47577

Library of Congress Catalog Number
99-72385

ISBN 0-87029-329-X

Printed in the United States of America

PrayerStarters

To Help You
Heal After Loss

by Elizabeth Stalling

ONE
CARING
PLACE

Abbey Press

Introduction

It's the hardest to pray when we hurt, it seems. What we want to do instead is yell and scream and moan and cry. What we don't realize is that these expressions, too, are prayers in themselves. As a matter of fact, these may be the only ways to pray after losing someone close to us. "Less-than-sweet" prayers are surely all God expects of us in our hardest times. And it is only by moving through grief that we can get beyond grief. That means letting our *feeling* prayers be *healing* prayers.

This small collection of PrayerStarters is just that: a collection of motivators and starters, to keep us on the way toward healing. They are intended to help us create prayer experiences and prayer expressions—and not just "prayer-words." Indeed, it is in expression and communication—whether giving or receiving—that all prayer happens. Thus included in this work are Scripture passages and quotations from many inspiring sources—all designed to help us find the words and the ways to express to God our sadness, anger, loneliness, guilt, and other painful feelings that come with grief.

These prayer-starters are also intended to help us listen to God. For indeed, so much of prayer is in the listening, the receiving, the paying attention, rather than in the speaking or "doing." Fortunately, "non-word" prayer seems to come easier and more naturally when we hurt. (Remember that great line in Ernest Hemingway's *The Old Man and the Sea*: "'Ay,' he said aloud. There is no translation for this word and perhaps it is just a noise such as a man might make, involuntarily, feeling the nail go through his hands and into the wood.") These prayer-starters, then, meet grievers "where they are": ready to pray such prayers as a prayer of tears, a prayer of anger, or a silent prayer of a soul feeling abandoned.

May the words and suggestions on these pages help get the healing started in our lives. May these words lift the reader's spirit, helping us to feel the presence of the God who is always listening, loving, and living the grief experience with us.

Making Small Beginnings

"Great peace is found in little busy-ness."
—Chaucer

"Nothing will ever be the same; that's the nature of loss. What you loved and were familiar with is not part of your life anymore. While facing the reality of 'nothing ever being the same,' go on to claim the rest of that reality: Things are different. With time, *very* different will be *somewhat* different—and with a little more time, *somewhat* different will become *fully familiar and normal.*"
—Kass Dotterweich, *Grieving as a Woman*

PrayerStarters

———⟋———

Think of a small prayer or gesture or ritual you can perform—something very personal and private and small. Maybe it's a Christian Sign of the Cross, or a short "Be with me, Lord," utterance. Or—perhaps it's a small religious object or sacred symbol to touch or grasp. These are the small prayers that get us on the way to healing. A small bow of the head may be appropriate as you pray:

You, Lord Jesus, started out your life small—a humble, lowly, "stable-boy." Help me to re-start my life with small, "baby steps." Here are some healing "first steps" I can take right now, with you at my side:

———————————   ———————————

Looking Ahead

"Get out your calendar and write down just how you plan to spend every Saturday and Sunday for the next month."
—Dr. Joyce Brothers

One philosopher has said that all we need are three things in life: Something to do, someone to love, something to look forward to. When we have suffered a loss, it seems that all three of these basic life requirements are taken away from us—or severely threatened. It's hard to remember that one of the "someones to love" is God. And that Someone continues to love us today, and will through every tomorrow.

PrayerStarters

It's time to take stock of what is left. Try to count the things that, with God's help, you can still do, the people you can still love (whether living or dead), the good things you can still look forward to. Name just a few of them here, and conclude with a simple prayer below:

_____   _____   _____

_____   _____   _____

Lord, you told us not to worry about tomorrow—to be like the birds of the air who have no concern about tomorrow. But, in truth, Lord, I'm more worried about today than tomorrow. Surround me, today, with your love. Help me, hold me, and see me through.

Reaching Out

"Without friends the world is but a wilderness...There is no man that imparteth his joys to his friends, but he joyeth the more; and no man that imparteth griefs to his friends, but he grieveth the less."
—Francis Bacon

Sometimes we need to hang on to someone else's strength, someone else's hope, someone else's peace or hope—while ours is under siege. Do it. Courage, strength, hope, faith, peace, and even sanity...they all come and go. Borrow them from someone else's supply until your own comes back to you.

There are rich reserves of all of these life necessities, if we but reach out for them.

PrayerStarters

Make an honest list of the people who have helped you the most thus far, and just what it was that really made the difference. "Sometimes the presence is all," goes a wise saying. Who are the people who have been most present to and for you? Write their names:

_____ _____ _____

Say the following prayer: Lord, you said "Blessed are those who mourn, for they shall be comforted." (Matthew 5:4) Well, I am mourning and in need of the comfort of friends, neighbors, co-workers, family, strangers—and you. May these good people—and you—be my comfort and my strength.

The Circle Will Be Unbroken

"Restoration is promised. That is the first and basic truth to hold onto. It doesn't take away the grief...but it does make it more endurable. The truth is that we will be reunited. My mother is in heaven now, and she is with my little brother who died. She lost him only for a time, and even though it was a long, sorrowful time, they are together again."
—David Knight, Catholic priest-author

"Failing to fetch me at first keep encouraged,
Missing me one place search another,
I stop somewhere waiting for you."

—Walt Whitman

PrayerStarters

Writer Leonard Foley reminds grievers that, "Within your love is a greater love. Beyond this world is another world. So do not get lost...and do not lose hope, either, at the bedside of your dying child, or in the multitude of insane tragedies your life may suffer. Look up! There is another world!"

Take a trip to the cemetery where loved ones are buried. Ask yourself what you believe about "Where are they now?" Ask God to bless the souls of all who have gone before us—and to strengthen our faith in the incomparable good that is to come for all who wait in hope and faith.

Honor the Memory

"You will not be cured, but...one day—an idea that will horrify you now—this intolerable misfortune will become a blessed memory of a being who will never again leave you."
—Marcel Proust

Yes, it can be painful to remember, but the very thought of forgetting someone we have loved so dearly is even more painful. So this is the time to remember, and to cherish the memories. The aim of our grief work is not to erase memories, but to make the painful memories less controlling. At the same time, preserving our good memories is part of the sacred trust left to us. We commit to cherish the shared love with which we have been so blessed. We pray that we may come to discover that we don't necessarily have to see what we love in order to know it is safe in our hearts.

PrayerStarters

It was Shakespeare who penned the beautiful thought: "But if the while I think on thee, dear friend, All losses are restored and sorrows end."

Perhaps the relationship you had with the one who has died was just this powerful and beautiful. If so, you will have many occasions to draw from your treasury of rich, life-giving memories. Keep in mind that it is just such a rich relationship that our loving God seeks with you, too. Take a moment to "think on God," and pray for the kind of loving relationship with God who can truly sustain you.

What Did I Do to Deserve This?

"It isn't raining on you; it's just raining."
—Anonymous

———————— 🍃 ————————

Sometimes we feel so hurt that we wonder if God isn't singling us out for pain, or specially targeting us because of something we did or did not do. We wonder just what we may have done wrong to deserve such suffering—or what our lost loved one did to "deserve" to suffer and die. In life we soon enough find out that what is fair and just, and what really happens, can be very, very different indeed. But God can stay with us through it all—if we stay with God.

PrayerStarters

As you try to think about God's view of our lives here on planet Earth, it's easy to conclude that "God must want us to suffer." But there are a host of great religious thinkers and teachers who tell us that God suffers with us; God grieves with us.

Meditate for a few moments on the following: Could it be that God is so close to you—embracing you, surrounding you, holding you in the hollow of loving hands—that you cannot see God? Is what you hear not only your own weeping—but God crying intimately, indiscernibly with you?

Express Yourself

"I am writing myself into well-being."
—From a personal journal

Writing—or telling people "how it was" and "how it is"—can be the best of therapies.

Writing Down Your Bones is the name of a popular book. It's about expressing one's essential, core feelings—one's very self, what's deep in the marrow of hurt. Expressing the hurt, writing it down, getting it out, is essential. It need not be literary or "publishable" material; the spellings and the grammar and the phraseology don't matter. It's time to get out the feelings.

PrayerStarters

Express honest feelings with these short prayers:

Dear Lord, I want to tell you just what's on my mind. These are the thoughts and words I need to say to you—some of them perhaps not so sweet and lovely. But I want to "Write Down My Bones" to you about what I am going through. You are my loving God, my loving friend, and I know you can take them! Here goes: _____

Dear Lord, if I were to imagine the words you want to be saying to me right now, they might include the following: _____

Praying Your Emptiness

"So I am allotted months of emptiness, and nights of misery are apportioned to me. When I lie down I say, 'When shall I rise?' But the night is long, and I am full of tossing until dawn."

—Job 7:3-4

"For now we see in a mirror, dimly, but then we will see face to face. Now I know only in part; then will I know fully, even as I have been fully known."

—I Corinthians 13:12

PrayerStarters

Make this a day to be honest about your loss and your feelings of emptiness and hurt. As you pray the following prayer, leave one small part of yourself open to new light and life—and the return, someday, of joy.

Dear God: No one told me I could hurt this much. I now know my life can never be the same again. Can it still be okay? You promised it would be when you said, "I have come that you may have life—and have it to the full." I'm not feeling very full right now; I'm feeling very empty. Show me the way to go from here. I don't even want a "full" life right now. I just want a life.

Holiday Miracles

*"Hold on to hope that, in one form or another,
the sparkle will one day return."*
– Karen Katafiasz

Getting through the holidays after experiencing a loss is a special challenge—and "celebrating" the holidays may seem like an impossibility. The key, now, is to do the holidays in a way that is right for you. Making prayer a bigger-than-usual part of the season may be one of the best responses. After all, you are probably feeling that only a miracle can get you through all this. And God does the best miracles. Ask for a simple miracle, in fervent prayer.

PrayerStarters

Meditate on these verses from a poem from Alfred Lord Tennyson. As you experience the grief the poet expresses, also ask God to help you experience a miracle of peace and calm in the midst of grief.

> Again at Christmas did we weave
> The holly round the Christmas hearth;
> The silent snow posses'd the earth,
> And calmly fell our Christmas eve.
>
> The yule-log sparkled keen with frost,
> No wing of wind the region swept,
> But over all things brooding slept
> The quiet sense of something lost.

The Courage to Heal

*"When you pass through the waters I will be with you:
and through the rivers, they shall not overwhelm you;
when you walk through fire you shall not be burned,
and the flame shall not consume you."*

—Isaiah 43:2

These familiar words from the Old Testament can be a testament to our courage—the personal courage it will take to weather the storm of loss. It's time now to remember that being courageous does not mean being unafraid; it means going ahead and doing what we must do despite all the fear in the world.

PrayerStarters

To pray for courage is to pray to "have heart"—to have the heart to get out of bed in the morning; to have the heart to be good to yourself when you're feeling your lowest; to have enough heart to still believe in love and happiness and joy after experiencing the depths of sadness and hurt...and heartlessness.

Lord, God, today I pray for heart. I pray to have the courage to love myself and life enough to do the following:_____

For those I love and those who love me:_____

For myself:_____

For you, God:_____

Take Care

*"Bereavement is a wound. It's like being
very, very badly hurt."*
—Lynn Caine, Widow

Healing from loss is like healing from radical surgery.
After all, a part of you has been ripped away. Just as the
body needs special treatment to recuperate, so your
broken heart needs special care to mend.

Consider your grieving time as an emotional convalescence. Go easy on yourself; take time off from "life as
usual." Since grieving is hard on both body and soul,
make sure you're eating healthy and getting as much
rest as possible. Be a patient patient: grieving takes
time.

PrayerStarters

Ask the Divine Healer for guidance on these questions:

- What "medicine" might ease your pain? What people, places, or activities have been healing for you in the past?
- Would it help to consult a "doctor of the soul," such as a clergyperson or other spiritual guide?
- Do you need to undertake any special "therapy"—like attending a Widow and Widowers group—to help you get back into circulation?
- What "Get Well" gifts might lift your spirits? Maybe you need to send yourself flowers (!) or ask a friend to bake you her famous lasagna.

Good Intentions

"I hear you stumbling for words. Relax. There are no words....You don't have to give me answers, for I will learn to live without them. You don't have to pretend my loved one never existed, thinking I will forget if you do. Let me speak his name, and you speak it, too. He is always there, that one I love so deeply, always part of who I am. If you take that from me, I will be less than who I am."

—Jacqueline L. Rogers, *I Want to Help But I Don't Know How*

Well-meaning people want to help but sometimes say the wrong things: "It's a blessing she went so quickly..." "He's better off now..." "You can always have another baby..." "It's God's will." Or they may pretend nothing has happened. It's okay to tell them gently and honestly what you need (or don't need) from them.

PrayerStarters

God helps those who help themselves...and those who accept help from others. You have prayed to God for comfort: your friends and family are God's answer to your prayer. Let them be God's arms to hold you, God's ears to listen to your sorrows, God's heart to simply be with you.

Call up someone who has offered help and tell that person what you need. Don't forget practical needs. Let someone bring you food or understanding, house-cleaning relief or the relief of tea and tears. God wants to comfort you through the goodness of the people around you.

The Ripple Effect

"Mourn not just for the loss of what was but also for what will never be."
—Karen Katafiasz, *Grief Therapy*

Losing someone close is not a one-fell-swoop blow. After the numbness wears off, after the shockwave of sadness knocks us to our knees, we come to another sobering realization: the hits just keep on coming—loss...after loss...after loss....

When someone close dies, it triggers a chain reaction. Not only is that person gone, but our shared dreams and goals are gone as well. The plans we had—never to happen. The hopes and possibilities—gone. The future we envisioned—not to be.

PrayerStarters

Just as we need to grieve the loss of our loved one, we also need to grieve the "secondary" losses. And in order to grieve them, we must first identify them. On separate slips of paper, write down the other losses resulting from your loved one's death.

Over the next few weeks, pray over each loss. Use the prayer of tears, the prayer of ranting and raving, the prayer of speechless sorrow...let the Spirit lead you. Then give each loss to God. You may want to symbolically let go by burning each slip of paper and letting the smoke rise to heaven.

Losing It

"Around you, life appears as usual. Yet nothing is the same. You eat, work, sleep—but you don't necessarily do them well....All the while, living seems devoid of purpose. There is something terribly, terribly wrong."

—Karen Katafiasz, *Finding Your Way Through Grief*

Your life has been tossed in the air, shattered and scattered into a million pieces. Somehow you go through the motions of living, but it's difficult to function. After all, what's the point? The most painful feelings you have ever experienced whirl inside you, a vortex of pain, sadness, anger, confusion. Meanwhile—and this is the greatest absurdity of all—everything around you runs just as it ever did: business as usual, the world still turns, life goes on. You must be going crazy.

PrayerStarters

Look upward for courage and then look outward—to others who understand what you're going through. Check into joining a bereavement support group. There, you won't feel like a stranger in a strange land, for those people travel the same rocky terrain as you. They can give you reassurance that losing it after losing someone is normal—and temporary.

"When it seems that our sorrow is too great to be borne, let us think of the great family of the heavy-hearted into which our grief has given us entrance, and, inevitably, we will feel about us their arms, their sympathy, their understanding."

—Helen Keller

Forging a New Bond of Heart and Spirit

"I have only slipped away into the next room....I am I, and you are you, and the old life that we lived so fondly together is untouched, unchanged. What we were to each other; that we are still. Call me by the old familiar name. Speak to me in that easy way you always used. Put no difference in your tone. Wear no false air of solemnity or sorrow. Laugh as we always laughed at the little jokes that we enjoyed together. Play, smile, think of me, pray for me....I am but waiting for you, for an interval somewhere, very near, just around the corner."

—Canon Henry Scott-Holland

PrayerStarters

Link spirits with your loved one in prayer:

Dear _____,

I miss you so much. I wish you were here with me right now. And, somehow, I know you are. Though my heart will always have an empty place inside it, I will furnish it with memories of the love we shared. You'll always live in me and I in you, and nothing can sever the bond between us.

Back to Nature

*"Deep contemplation of beauty...is still our most creative
human response to the shredding of a soul."*
—Phil Cousineau, *The Soul of the World*

A scarlet cardinal against the backdrop of
winter...the welcome tender green of spring shoots...
the spatter of brilliant stars on a clear night...the brilliant
palette of sunset. The beauty of nature soothes our spirits; the grandeur of nature witnesses to the majesty and
mystery of the Creator.

PrayerStarters

Go outdoors to a spot where you feel in tune with nature. If you can't get there in reality, escape there in your imagination. Stop...look...listen... feel. Soak in the serenity. Let nature's beauty and power seam your raveled soul.

Reflect on the rhythms of nature, the seasonal cycles of death and rebirth. Look for evidence of the infinite variety of nature, its intricate and elaborate laws, and the vastness of the universe. Do these discoveries give you any new insights into your grief experience? Into the nature of God?

Read Job: 38–39.

Wounded Healer

"Can I see another's woe,
And not be in sorrow, too?
Can I see another's grief,
And not seek for kind relief?"
—William Blake

You never knew you could hurt this much. And as you reel from the pain of your loss, your thoughts inevitably turn to others: the friend whose brother committed suicide, the neighbor with a chronic illness, the co-worker who suffered multiple deaths in her family. Though you certainly felt sympathy before, you now know much more intimately how they feel. Your grief has carved out a special place in your heart that, though tender, has given you entry into the pain of suffering people everywhere.

PrayerStarters

Dear God,

In my suffering, you have given me new compassion for others' suffering. Forgive me and let me forgive myself for not having been as sensitive in the past as I might have been. Help me to use this new, hard-won vision to see the suffering of the people I encounter every day. Inspire me to offer a listening ear or a shoulder to cry on or a helping hand. Amen.

In the next week, try to make some kind of a personal contribution to ease the pain of suffering humanity—for example, a financial donation, volunteer service, or a letter to advocate for a more humane public policy.

Hope Springs Eternal

"Hope is both a gift and a choice.
We ask for it and choose to act it."
—Bonnie O. Miller

Time passes...and grief is no longer your constant companion—it leaves you for a few minutes, an hour, a day. You still remember your love, of course, and the hole in your heart still hurts, but bit by bit you find yourself beginning to look forward more than back, to hope for hope.

Be alert to these first signs of springtime in your soul; cultivate every tender bud of hope. It's not a betrayal of your loved one's memory to feel good again—wouldn't he or she want that for you? Open up (you've been squeezed tight against the onslaught of death and grief); embrace all life has to offer.

PrayerStarters

Plant a flower or tree as a living memorial to your loved one and pray:

Dear God,
I dedicate this plant in honor of _____.
As it weathers the seasons, may it remind me of the natural rhythms of death and rebirth, the spring within every winter, the promise of new life within every pang of grief.

I choose to believe that you can transform death into life, brokenness into blessedness. I open my heart and lie in wait for the new beginning you have in store for me.

To Accept the Things I Cannot Change

"Acceptance doesn't mean giving up. It means giving all—our sorrow, anger, powerlessness—to God. It means peering into the emptiness to discover the divine spark that can never be extinguished. It means believing God's love and wisdom prevail over every moment of existence."

—Lisa Engelhardt

We can cry and feel some release, but it doesn't change things. We can scream "Why?" but we never get a real answer. We can tell our story over and over, but it doesn't take away the source of the pain. There is no answer or solution to, no reversal of this thing called death. Ultimately, we must come to acceptance.

PrayerStarters

Meditate on this text:

"We want to be healed, we want to mend the broken pieces of our souls, we want the cup of suffering to pass from us, yet it is not to be. Instead, we are to ask for one thing only—true surrender of our being to God....With this surrender comes the light that guides us on the path of the spirit; and with this surrender comes a faith in, not a God of rescue and restoration, but a God who would love and live in us, even through our trials and tribulations."

—Adolfo Quezada, *Through the Darkness*

In God I Trust

"*Little by little, God's goodness—visible in other people, in the world, in myself—became too apparent for me to ignore or deny. And I began to trust life again. That, after all, is what it comes down to—trust. Trust that life doesn't end with death. Trust that loved ones who have died are forever with God and that God is forever with us, too.*"

—Robert DiGiulio, from the CareNote *Losing Someone Close*

"My friend, you belong to God. Let this reality color your entire existence. Give yourself up to God ceaselessly with every beat of your heart."

—St. Vincent de Paul

PrayerStarters

Sit quietly and focus on your breathing. Breathe in deeply...breathe out slowly. In...out...the rhythm of life. With every breath we take, God sustains us. Then pray:

God, I believe...
that you know and want only what's best for me;
that in my grief you hold me close to your heart,
    a heart that holds all the sorrows of the world;
that the world is still a good place;
that my life still has purpose;
that death is just a horizon beyond which I cannot see;
that one day I will be reunited with my loved one in a place of eternal joy.

I Once Was Lost...

"Have mercy on me, Lord, I have no strength."
—Psalm 6

It's a terrifying experience to be lost. We rely on all kinds of "landmarks" to help us know we have not lost our way in life: home, family, relationships, the order of daily life. When we suffer loss, it's as if the things that used to help us find our way look different, or have even disappeared. Through it all, even if our very relationship with God seems different or uncertain, God nevertheless continues to reach out to us. When we wander like children lost in a department store, filled with fright and shock, God is like a mother, diligently scanning each aisle, seeking us out to comfort and reassure us.

PrayerStarters

Reflect on a moment when you felt lost—as a child, on vacation, in the confusion of adolescence.

What helped you find your way? Who helped you find your way?

Know that God wants to help you overcome the disorientation you are feeling right now.

Dear God,
When I am lost, help me find my way. When I am tired, be my strength.
When I am frightened, be my comfort.

You'll Never Walk Alone

"Solitude is bearable only with God."
—André Gide

"It's not just that I lost my fishing buddy," a recently widowed man said, "I've lost a part of me." The loneliness that is often a result of loss is much deeper than merely missing someone who used to be present; it's also missing a part of you, a part of life itself. The sense of isolation that can arise from such a realization can be nearly crippling.

In the midst of it all, even if we cannot always see or feel it, God is with us; we really are not alone. While no one can make the loneliness go away, there is one who shares our suffering and solitude. Recognizing this presence can lessen the impact of loneliness on our lives.

PrayerStarters

Dear God,

Help me to be aware of your presence in my life. Help me to see you in the kindness of neighbors and friends, in the concern of family. Help me to hear you in the words of comfort that others speak. Help me to feel you in a kind touch, a supportive hug.

I feel so alone. Help me to know that you are with me.

Yell—God Can Take It!

"Will the Lord reject us for ever?
Will he show us his favor no more?
Has his love vanished for ever?"

—Psalm 76

A natural human response to suffering on any scale is to lay blame somewhere, even on God. "Why are you doing this to me?" "What did I do to deserve this?" In the midst of suffering, it can be not only natural, but almost comforting, to blame God for our sorrow.

This "blaming of God" is a prayer itself. When we blame God for things, we are acknowledging that God is active and present in our lives, even if we misunderstand God's ways. Whenever we are aware of God's presence, prayer is happening.

PrayerStarters

Do you want to blame God for anything?

Are God's ways confusing to you?

Go ahead and say what your heart is telling you to say—God can take it.

Dear God,
Sometimes I want to blame you for all of the things that have happened to me, all of the sorrows in my life. Thank you for taking it from me, for listening to my complaints.

Anger Therapy

"Anger cannot be dishonest."
—George R. Bach

Anger is a natural element of the human condition; everyone has been angry at one time or another. While there is destructive anger, (like chewing out the driver who has cut us off in traffic), there is also righteous anger (like the anger aroused by real injustice).

The anger that comes to the surface after a loss is significant and real. We can become angry at health care professionals, family members, well-intentioned friends, God, even the person we grieve. All of this is natural, honest anger, but needs to be appropriately expressed so that it doesn't hurt ourselves or others.

PrayerStarters

Dear God,
   Right now, I am feeling angry at _____.
It seems unfair to me that _____
had to happen. Send me your healing spirit so that this
anger will not achieve too great a power over my life.
Let your power conquer the anger, and heal my soul.

Depression

*"How long must I bear grief in my soul,
this sorrow in my heart day and night?"*
—Psalm 12

Depression often accompanies grief and loss. Our heart aches with loss as we are surrounded by the reminders of our loved one, whom we miss so much. There are even times when depression can be so intense that we need to get professional help to deal with it.

God understands our sorrows; God weeps with us. Knowing that, feeling that, will not necessarily make depression go away, but it can lessen its grip on us.

PrayerStarters

Dear God,

   My loss fills me with sadness. In the midst of my sorrow, help me to know that your goodness is there, even if I can't see or feel it right now. Embrace me with your love, so that my heart may be freed from its sorrow.

Laugh, and the World Laughs With You

"Laughter is the closest thing to the grace of God."
—Karl Barth

There is something truly healing about laughter. A good joke, a funny story, our own stumblings and bumblings—being aware of the humorous elements in life can free our minds from oppressive sorrow, quicken steps made slow by loss, and lift the burden of grief from our shoulders.

Sometimes we may feel that it is inappropriate to laugh in the midst of grief, but it is precisely in the most un-funny times of our life that laughter can have its most powerful, healing effect.

PrayerStarters

Do something that will make you laugh: reflect on a funny story, rent your favorite comedy, read an old comic book, share a joke with a friend.

Reflect on what an amazing gift from God that your laughter is.

Imagine that, if only for a moment, God's joyful presence is replacing your loss.

Dear God,
Thank you for your gift of laughter. Help me, as I heal from loss, to see the joy that is present in life.

...Forgive Us

"How unhappy is he who cannot forgive himself."
—Publilius Syrus, *Moral Sayings*

"If only I had...I should have...Why didn't I?..." When suffering loss the questions and "what-if's" can be maddening. We can so question events, so wonder about how things could have been different, that we begin to take on guilt for things that were really beyond our control.

No one is perfect, and mistakes may have been made, but blaming ourselves for any tragedy in our life ultimately does nothing but weigh us down with unnecessary burdens. Recognize in the beginnings of self-forgiveness an important step in the journey to wholeness, to healing.

PrayerStarters

Dear God,
    I am feeling guilty because of _____.
Help me to know and understand the limitations of my humanity. When I am impatient with myself, send me patience. When I am angry with myself, send me love. When I feel guilty, send me forgiveness. May this patience, love, and forgiveness soothe my troubled soul.

...As We Forgive Those

"We pardon as long as we love."
—Rochefoucauld, *Maxims*

Suffering a loss can bring about a great deal of anger and blame. We may blame health care professionals, or friends, or even our lost loved one. Unchecked, all of this can so accumulate that we spend too much time blaming, and not enough time healing.

While this blaming is a natural part of grieving, forgiveness is a necessary and vital step as well. When anger and confusion darken our vision, it is only through the act of forgiving that the true light of love can begin to penetrate that darkness.

PrayerStarters

Who in your life do you need to forgive? For what?

Write a letter to someone you want to forgive. Let the reality of love strengthen your hand to let go of the hurt. Putting the thoughts on paper can help you, even if you don't send the letter.

Dear God,
Help me to forgive, as I have been forgiven. Lead me from the bondage of anger and resentment to the freedom of love.

Suffering

"Man is born broken. He lives by mending. The grace of God is glue."
—Eugene O'Neill, *The Great God Brown*

"Why?" countless people have cried out in pain—to God, to others—striving to make sense of the suffering that is a part of the human existence, a sad reality in the world. But "why's" cannot always be answered, our suffering often doesn't make sense.

Even if we cannot grasp the mystery of human suffering, we can begin to see the results of it. As steel is tempered by fire, as trees grow livelier through pruning, as backs grow stronger after carrying heavy loads, so suffering can temper, enliven, and strengthen us.

PrayerStarters

Dear God,

I don't always understand the things in this world that cause me to suffer. I grapple with questions of "Why," and I am confused when I don't always hear answers.

Help me to see that the mysterious revelation of your love is present even in the mist of my suffering. Help me to know what I can learn from my suffering. Strengthen my back to carry the load.

Saying Goodbye

"Ever has it been that love knows not its own depth until the hour of separation."
—Kahlil Gibran, *The Prophet*

Saying goodbye is never easy, and saying goodbye for good is even more difficult. It's natural for us to want those we love to remain with us always. Acknowledging that someone is gone forever is a very painful part of the grieving process.

Although saying goodbye is an act of separation, the depth of love insures that some things continue forever, through memories, through events, through other people. Saying goodbye doesn't mean letting go of all of this; it means, rather, recognizing both that which has been taken from us and that which can never be taken from us.

PrayerStarters

Dear God,

I am having difficulty saying goodbye. Help me to let go of what is gone, while still clinging to that which will be with me always. May the depth of your love help fill what is empty, and help me to know that I am never truly alone.

Being Grateful

*"The highest tribute to the dead
is not grief, but gratitude."*
—Thornton Wilder

———————— ✿ ————————

It is no secret that love is stronger than death. That is something to celebrate. The life you shared with the one who has died is also something to celebrate, to remember, to be thankful for. Don't hide the hope and joy you may eventually feel that your loved one now is in a place of eternal joy.

PrayerStarters

Your fondest wish at this time—if complete restoration and reunion has to wait—is that God now blesses your loved one with peace and joy beyond all human understanding.

Meditate for just a few moments on the Christian creed that "Eye has not seen nor ear heard" what God has prepared for us after our earthly life has ended.

Conclude with a prayer of gratitude for the gift of life—and the Gift of Love.

About the Author

Elizabeth Stalling is a wife and mother of three children, two dogs, and a cat. Her hobbies include ceramics, cinema, and hiking. This is her first book.

PrayerStarters Series

————— ✑ —————

- *PrayerStarters in Times of Pain or Illness*
  by Alaric Lewis, O.S.B. #20110

- *PrayerStarters to Help You Handle Stress*
  by Molly Wigand #20107

- *PrayerStarters for Busy People*
  by Daniel Grippo #20109

- *PrayerStarters to Help You Heal After Loss*
  by Elizabeth Stalling #20108

Available at your favorite bookstore or gift shop, or
directly from: One Caring Place, Abbey Press,
St. Meinrad, IN 47577
(800) 325-2511